You might be from Saskatchewan if...

CARSON DEMMANS
JASON SYLVESTRE

MacIntyre Purcell Publishing Inc.
PO Box 1142
Lunenburg, Nova Scotia
B0J 2C0
(902) 640-2337
www.macintyrepurcell.com
info@macintyrepurcell.com

Cover design: Channel Communications
Inside layout design: Channel Communications

Printed and bound in Canada by Marquis book printing.

Demmans, Carson   You might be from Saskatchewan if-- / Carson Demmans, Jason Sylvestre.

Also issued in electronic format. ISBN 978-1-927097-21-2

     1. Saskatchewan--Social life and customs--Caricatures and cartoons. 2. Canadian wit and humor, Pictorial. 3. Comic books, strips, etc. I. Sylvestre, Jason II. Title.

FC3511.3.D44 2012   741.5'971   C2012-904272-2

We acknowledge the support of the Department of Canadian Heritage and the Nova Scotia Department of Tourism, Culture and Heritage in the development of writing and publishing in Canada.

 Canadian Heritage   Patrimoine canadien    NOVA SCOTIA    Canada

FOREWORD

Regina, Saskatchewan. I don't know why but just thinking of Carson's hometown always makes me chuckle. Mispronouncing it is even funnier!

Isn't it weird that such a square (actually Saskatchewan is more rectangular, of course) place would produce such a number of wacky comedy writers?

Carson has been a steady and funny contributor of many of the better gags in my daily comic strip "PC & Pixel," first syndicated by the Washington Post Writers' Group at the start of this millennium.

And here in *You Might Be From Saskatchewan If...* he is hilarious in this self examination of his home province.

— **Tak Bui**

INTRODUCTION

There is no such thing as a typical resident of Saskatchewan. There is a huge, wonderful variation in ethnic background, language, occupation and age in this odd rectangle of a place. Everyone who lives here is different from their neighbour in some way.

But, Saskatchewanians all have something in common: they all have a good sense of humor . . . a Saskatchewan sense of humour, a humour capable of appreciating the small detail of everyday life.

Saskatchewan is a place of extraordinary variation. The temperature can and do go from -40 to plus 40. The land can be anything from unending trees and lakes to a sea of grass. In summer, you can see everything from drought to flooding, and all within a matter of days. Tornadoes may strike or the air may be calm for days.

Anything can happen here, and it is usually beyond the control of anyone. But, when it does, people get up, dust themselves off (and we have a lot of dust here), and get on with their lives. In a few months, everyone is making jokes about the tornado or the plague of locusts or whatever else caused a temporary inconvenience earlier. People live, people laugh. Welcome to Saskatchewan.

If you are from Saskatchewan, we hope you will recognize things in this book that remind you of people you know or used to know, and maybe even yourself. This book is ultimately a tribute to this crazy, unusual place and especially to the people in it, people who used to live here, and those who may live here in the future.

It has been great fun doing this book. We hope you have as much fun reading it.

Enjoy.

— Carson Demmans, Jason Sylvestre

This book is dedicated to my loving wife Shelley, who proves she has a great sense of humour everytime she sticks with me for one more day.

— Carson Demmans

Dedicated to my wife and kids, with out their support I could not do things like this, also dedicatd to my fellow Saskatchewanians, Go Riders!!

— Jason Sylvestre

The Journey Begins . . .

YOU CONSIDER ONE CABBAGE ROLL AND SIX TYPES
OF PEROGIES TO BE A SEVEN COURSE MEAL.

YOU GET NOSEBLEEDS IN HIGHER ALTITUDES.

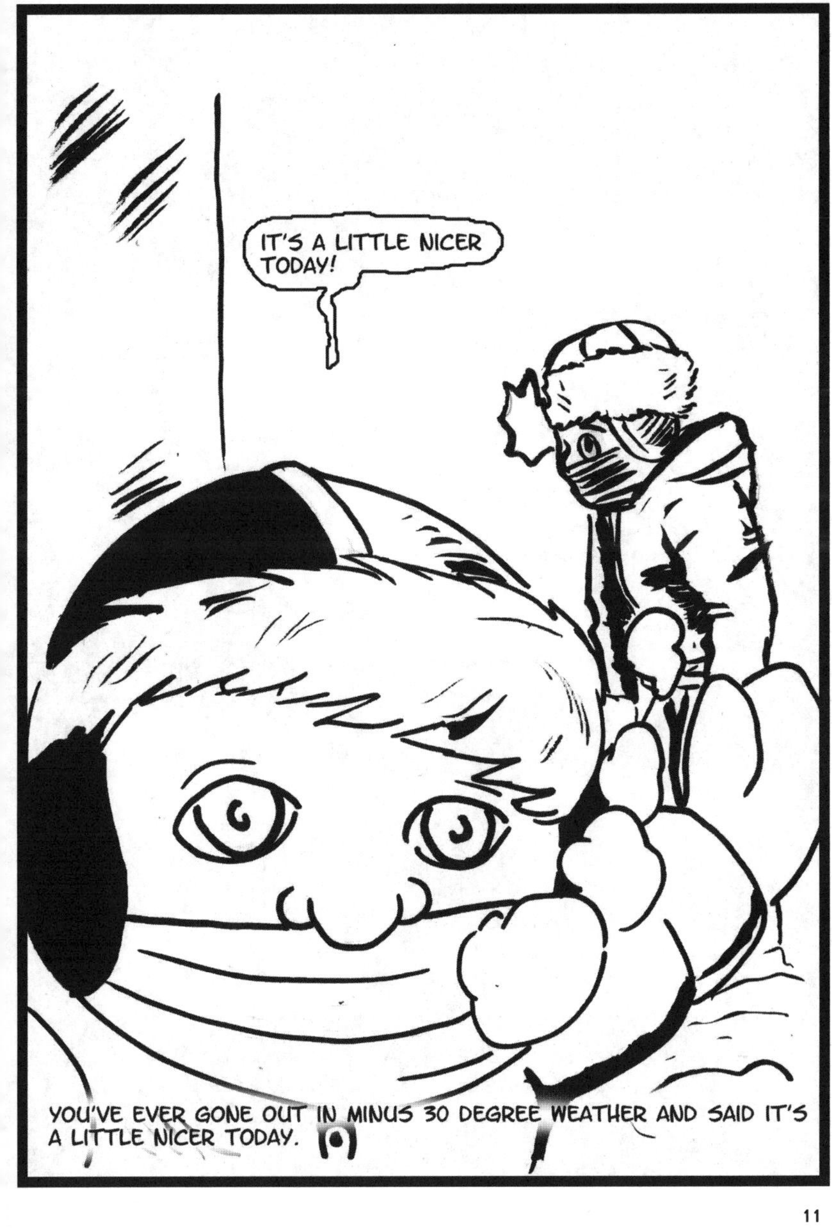
IT'S A LITTLE NICER TODAY!
YOU'VE EVER GONE OUT IN MINUS 30 DEGREE WEATHER AND SAID IT'S A LITTLE NICER TODAY.

1966

1989   **2001**

GREY CUP CHAMPS!

YOU CONSIDER 23 YEARS BETWEEN PROFESSIONAL SPORTS CHAMPIONSHIPS ACCEPTABLE.

YOU CONSIDER 3 MILES OF VISABILITY TO BE A LITTLE FOGGY.

YOU HAVE FALLEN ASLEEP AT THE WHEEL KNOWING THERE ARE NO CURVES ON THE ROAD FOR AT LEAST HALF AN HOUR.

YOU NEVER GET TIRED OF THE, "BUT THIS IS BIGGAR" JOKE.

YOU CONSIDER A HALF TON TRUCK TO BE A FUEL EFFICIENT COMPACT.

YOU HAVE GONE TO THE MARITIMES AND NEEDED A TRANSLATOR.

YOU READ THE CONSTITUTION AND WERE SURPRISED TO FIND OUT THAT UKRANIAN IS NOT AN OFFICIAL LANGUAGE.

YOU WROTE A PROTEST LETTER TO THE CBC FOR
SUGGESTING THAT TOMMY DOUGLAS MIGHT NOT BE
THE GREATEST CANADIAN.

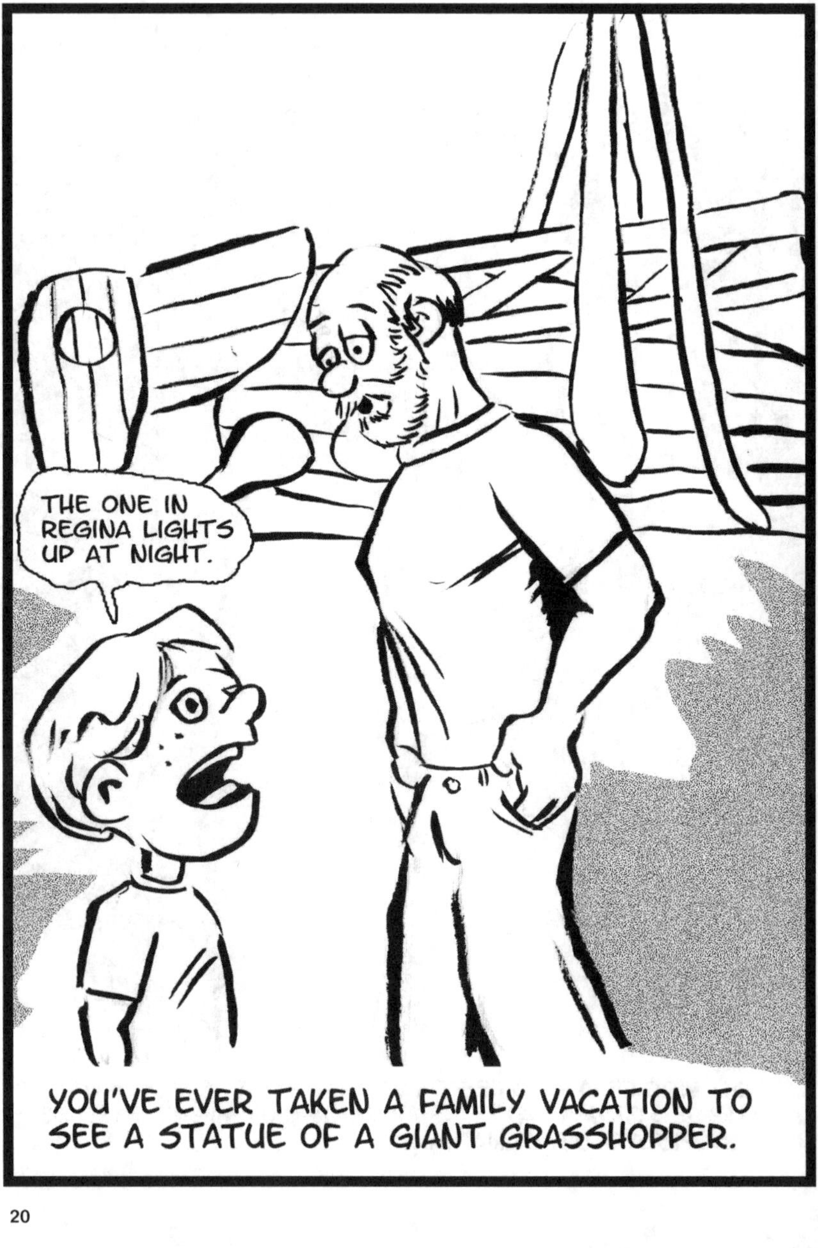
THE ONE IN REGINA LIGHTS UP AT NIGHT.
YOU'VE EVER TAKEN A FAMILY VACATION TO SEE A STATUE OF A GIANT GRASSHOPPER.

YOUR EMPLOYER ALLOWS YOU TIME OFF TO HARVEST GRAIN.

YOUR GOLF CART HAS SNOW TIRES.

YOU DON'T ACKNOWLEDGE ANY PRIME MINISTERS
AFTER DIEFENBAKER.

YOU HAVE A RELATIVE WHO ONCE BOUGHT A SECOND PICK UP TRUCK BECAUSE THE GUN RACK IN HIS FIRST ONE WAS FULL.

YOU'VE USED A COW PATTY AS SECOND BASE.

YOU HAVE HAD MORE DEER IN YOUR YARD THAN THE AVERAGE ZOO.

YOU HAVE EVER USED FOUR WHEEL DRIVE
TO GET OUT OF A POT HOLE.

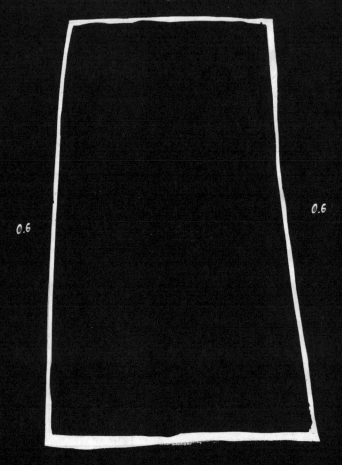

YOU HAVE DRAWN A PROVINCIAL MAP IN
UNDER THREE SECONDS.

YOUR PARENTS STILL REMEMBER WHEN POWER WAS INSTALLED.

YOU HAVE EVER PROPOSED GORDIE HOWE FOR SAINTHOOD.

YOU HAVE DRIVEN IN TORONTO AND SHOOK
FOR A WEEK AFTERWARDS.

YOU HAVE EVER LEASH TRAINED A GOPHER.

YOU HAVE EVER SAID "NICE RACK" TO A MAN.

YOU HAVE EVER WHISTLED AT A GIRL WEARING A PARKA AND SNOW BOOTS.

YOU HAVE EVER GOTTEN INTO A FIST FIGHT WITH AN EASTERNER OVER HOW TO PRONOUNCE THE LETTERS W-A-N.

YOUR GRADUATING CLASS ARRIVED AT THE CEREMONY IN ONE CAR.

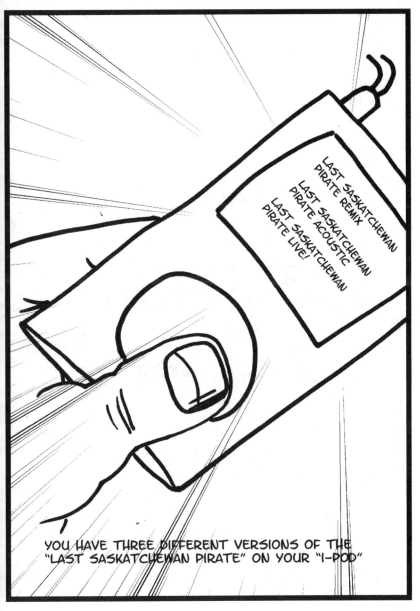

YOU HAVE THREE DIFFERENT VERSIONS OF THE "LAST SASKATCHEWAN PIRATE" ON YOUR "I-POD"

YOU REFER TO ANY POINT IN-BETWEEN PRINCE ALBERT AND THE U.S. BORDER AS THE SOUTH.

YOUR SECOND CAR IS A SNOWMOBILE.

YOU HAVE GONE TO A WEDDING AND
BEEN RELATED TO BOTH SIDES.

YOU HAVE EATEN ALL 3 MEALS IN ONE DAY AT A DONUT SHOP

41

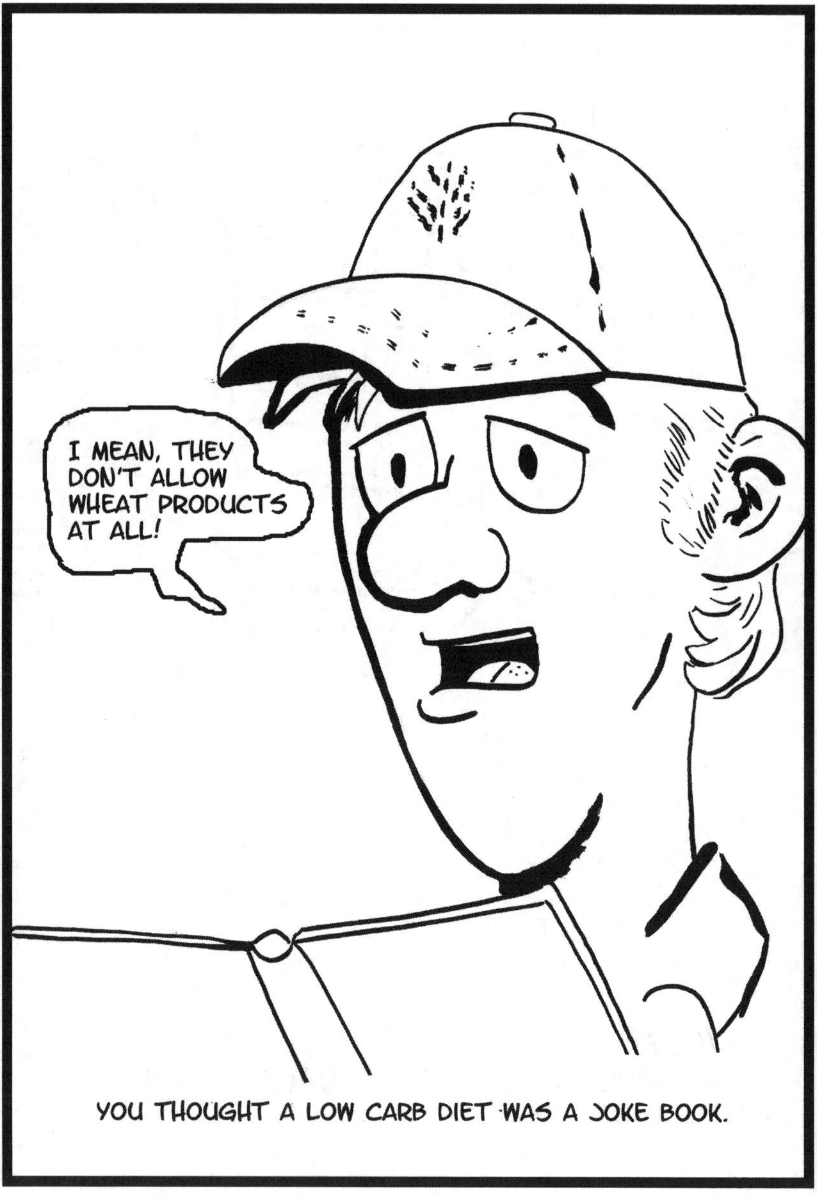
I MEAN, THEY DON'T ALLOW WHEAT PRODUCTS AT ALL!
YOU THOUGHT A LOW CARB DIET WAS A JOKE BOOK.

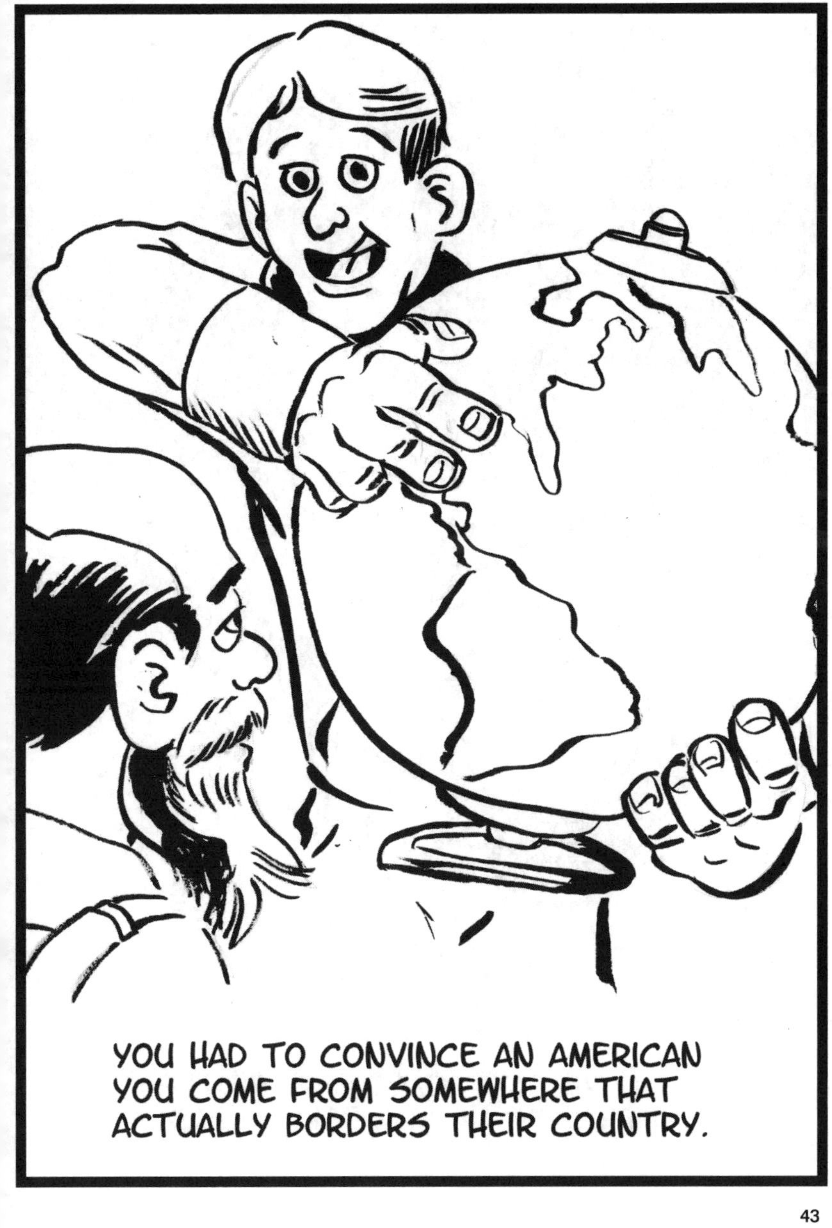
YOU HAD TO CONVINCE AN AMERICAN
YOU COME FROM SOMEWHERE THAT
ACTUALLY BORDERS THEIR COUNTRY.

YOU HAVE PETITIONED THE WINTER OLYMPICS TO HAVE A POKER DERBY.

YOU DON'T KNOW WHO JERRY SEINFELD IS BUT
YOU HAVE SEEN NESTOR PISTER 23 TIMES.

YOU HAVE COMPETED IN A SPORT THAT HAS AN ASH TRAY FOR EVERY TEAM AND A BAR FOR ALL COMPETITORS.

YOU MOVE TO A BIG CITY OUT OF PROVINCE
AND YOU SUDDENLY HAVE A LOT OF FRIENDS
FROM HIGH SCHOOL VISITING WEEKLY

YOU STILL HAVE A "SASKATOON BLUES" JERSEY

YOU HAVE LIVED IN THE CITY YOUR WHOLE LIFE, AND YOU CAN STILL IDENTIFY CROPS AS YOU DRIVE BY THEM ON THE HIGHWAY.

YOU STILL HAVE THE SHANNON TWEED
ISSUE OF PLAYBOY.

YOU STILL REMEMBER WHERE YOU WERE
WHEN THE RIDERS LOST THE 1976 GREY CUP.

YOU HAVE FORMAL AND CASUAL BASEBALL CAPS.

YOU HAVE EVER NAVIGATED USING
GRAIN ELEVATORS AS LANDMARKS.

YOU HAD TO PICK UP YOUR KIDS FROM SCHOOL BECAUSE THE SNOW WAS TOO DEEP FOR THE SCHOOL BUSES TO GET THROUGH.

YOU STILL HOPE FOR A QUEEN CITY KIDS REUNION.

YOU CAN DRIVE THROUGH SMUTS, SEMANS AND CLIMAX WITHOUT GIGGLING.

YOU KNOW WHERE BUFFY ST. MARIE AND JOANIE MITCHELL WERE BORN BUT YOU CAN'T IDENTIFY ANY OF THEIR SONGS.

YOU WENT TO A SCHOOL WHERE GUN SAFETY WAS ONE OF THE CLASSES THAT WAS OFFERED.

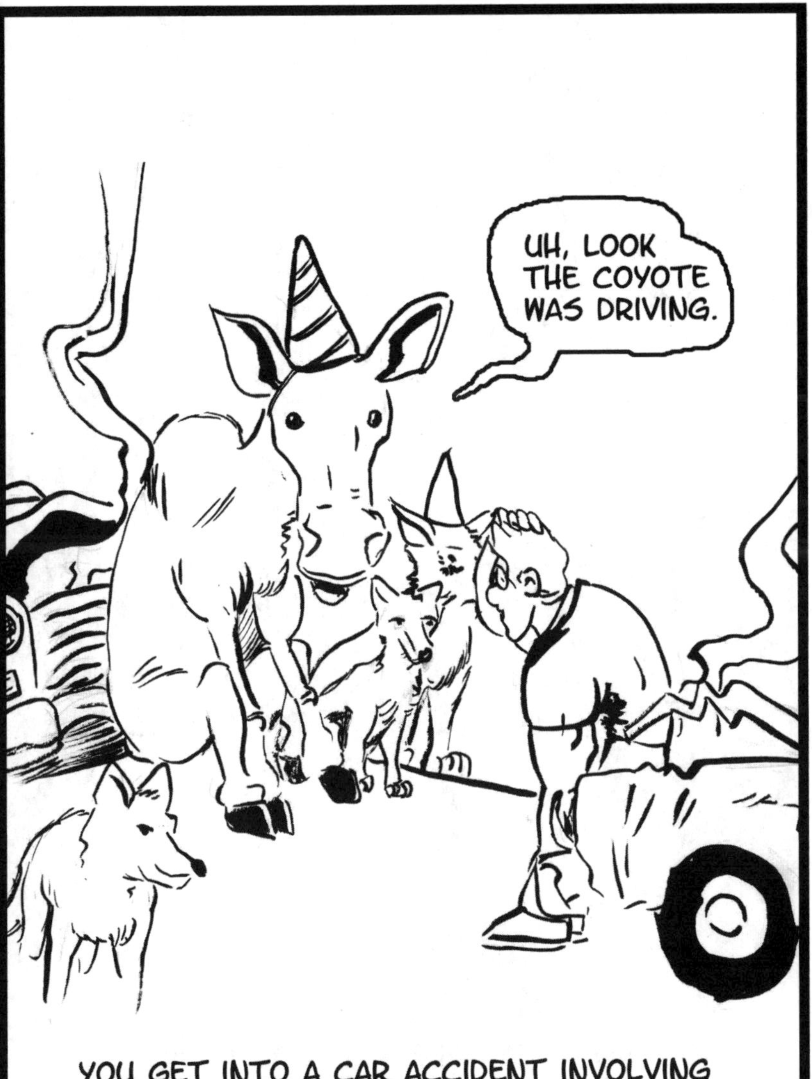
UH, LOOK THE COYOTE WAS DRIVING.
YOU GET INTO A CAR ACCIDENT INVOLVING A MOOSE, TWO COYOTES AND A WOLF AND SAY "NOT AGAIN".

YOU INVITE PEOPLE YOU DON'T LIKE FROM TORONTO TO VISIT YOU BECAUSE YOU KNOW THEY WILL NEVER SHOW.

A BAND THAT HAD ONE TOP 40 HIT 20 YEARS AGO IS FINALLY PLAYING YOUR HOME TOWN NEXT WEEK.

YOU LIVE IN A CITY THAT HAD TO BUILD
EITHER A HILL OR A LAKE.

YOU HAVE EVER BOUGHT CHILDREN'S TOYS AT A FARM IMPLEMENT DEALER.

YOU HAVE LIVED IN A TOWN WHERE THE COMBINED VALUE OF ALL OF THE HOUSES WOULD STILL BE LESS THAN THE COST OF A ONE BEDROOM CONDO IN VANCOUVER.

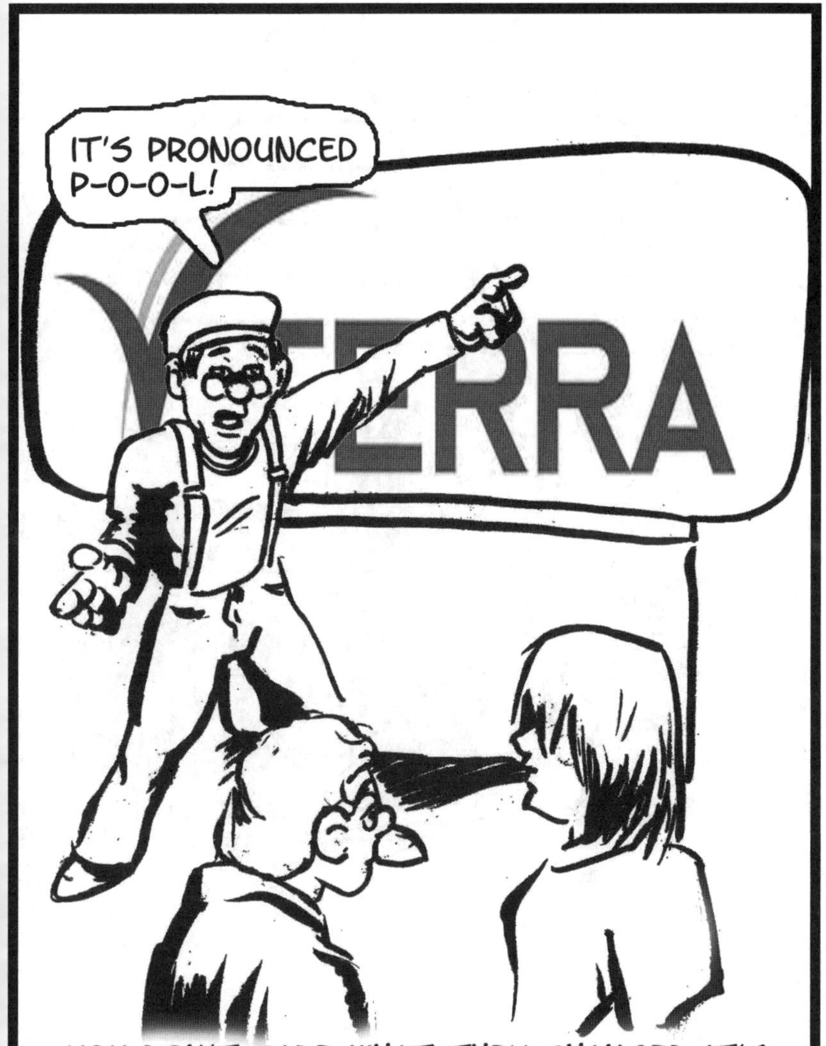
IT'S PRONOUNCED P-O-O-L!
VTERRA

YOU DON'T CARE WHAT THEY CHANGED IT'S NAME TO. TO YOU IT WILL ALWAYS BE THE WHEAT POOL.

YOUR SNOWBLOWER HAS MORE HORSEPOWER
THAN YOUR CAR.

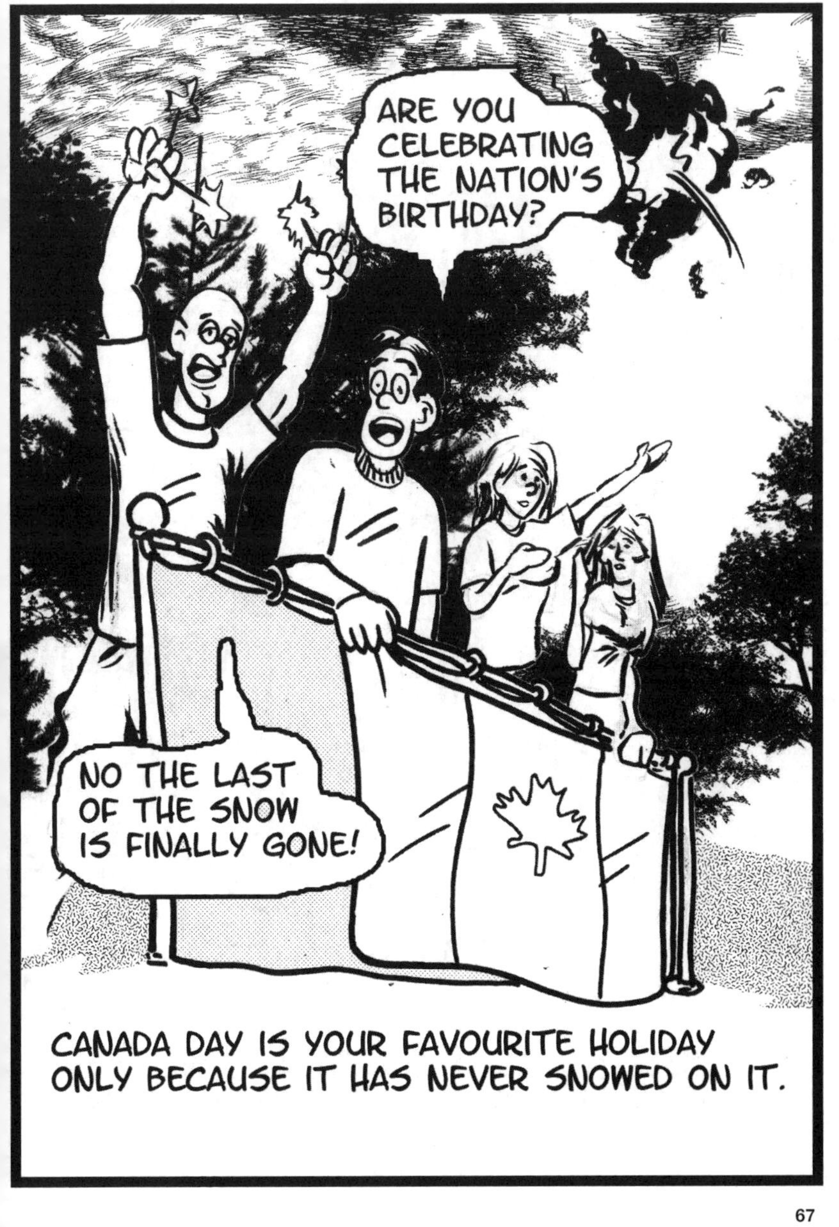
ARE YOU CELEBRATING THE NATION'S BIRTHDAY?
NO THE LAST OF THE SNOW IS FINALLY GONE!

CANADA DAY IS YOUR FAVOURITE HOLIDAY ONLY BECAUSE IT HAS NEVER SNOWED ON IT.

YOU ONCE SCORED A GOAL IN A HOCKEY GAME BY BANKING A SHOT OFF OF A PASSING CAR.

YOU HAVE SEEN LITTLE MOSQUE ON THE PRARIE, BUT MISTAKE IT FOR A DOCUMENTARY.

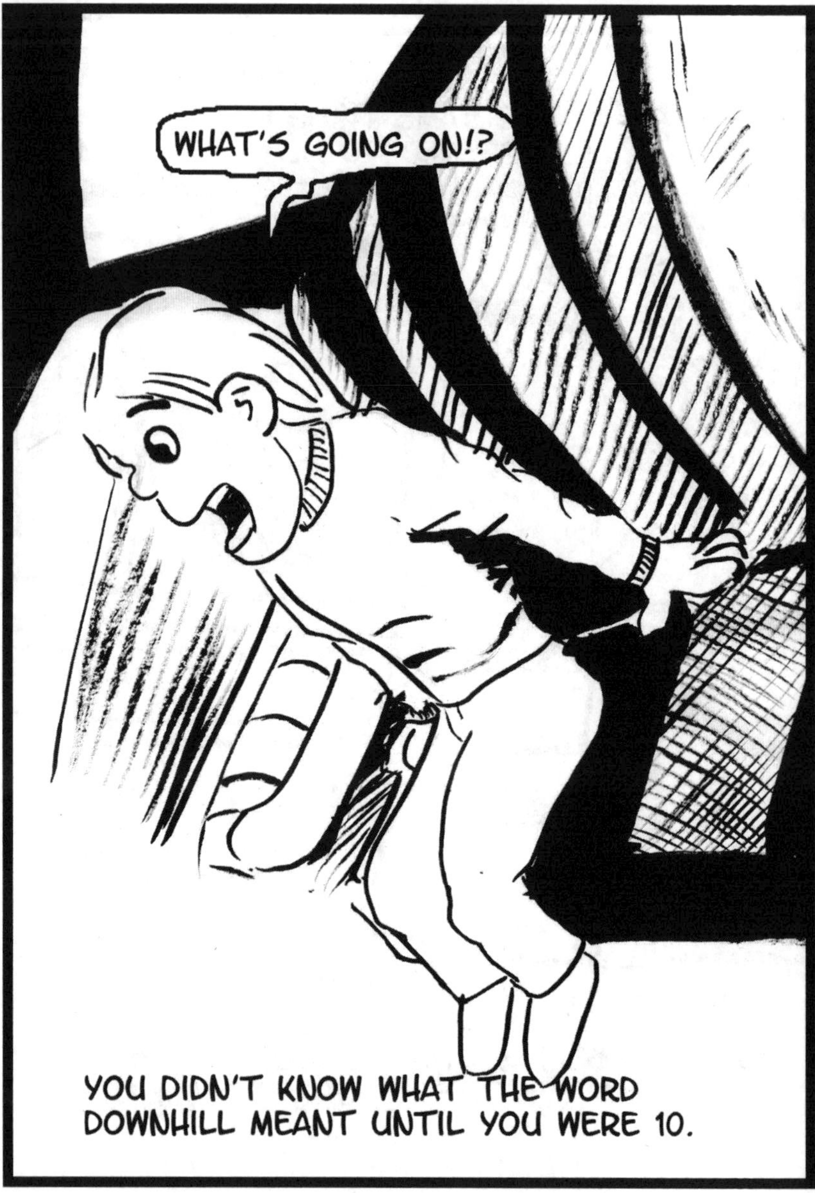
WHAT'S GOING ON!?
YOU DIDN'T KNOW WHAT THE WORD DOWNHILL MEANT UNTIL YOU WERE 10.

YOU HAVE WORN OUT A SNOW SHOVEL.

WHEN YOU GO TO A FANCY EVENT IN THE
WINTER, YOU MAKE SURE TO WEAR YOUR
FORMAL LONG UNDERWEAR.

YOU HAVE HEARD ABOUT GLOBAL WARMING:
YOU JUST DON'T CONSIDER IT TO BE A
BAD THING.

SOMEONE TELLS YOU THEY ARE FROM THE DEEP SOUTH AND YOU ASSUME THEY MEAN SWIFT CURRENT.

YOU SEE FOOTAGE OF GANG VIOLENCE ON TELEVISION AND MISTAKE IT FOR HIGHLIGHTS OF A WHL GAME.

YOU HAVE USED A BASEBALL BAT AS A FLY SWATTER.

YOUR FAMILY'S WINTER HOME IS AN
ICE FISHING SHACK.

YOU'VE HAD TO BUY A NEW THERMOMETER BECAUSE THE OLD ONE DIDN'T GO DOWN FAR ENOUGH.

YOU HAVE CHEERED A ROAD CONSTRUCTION CREW FOR COMPLETING REPAIRS.

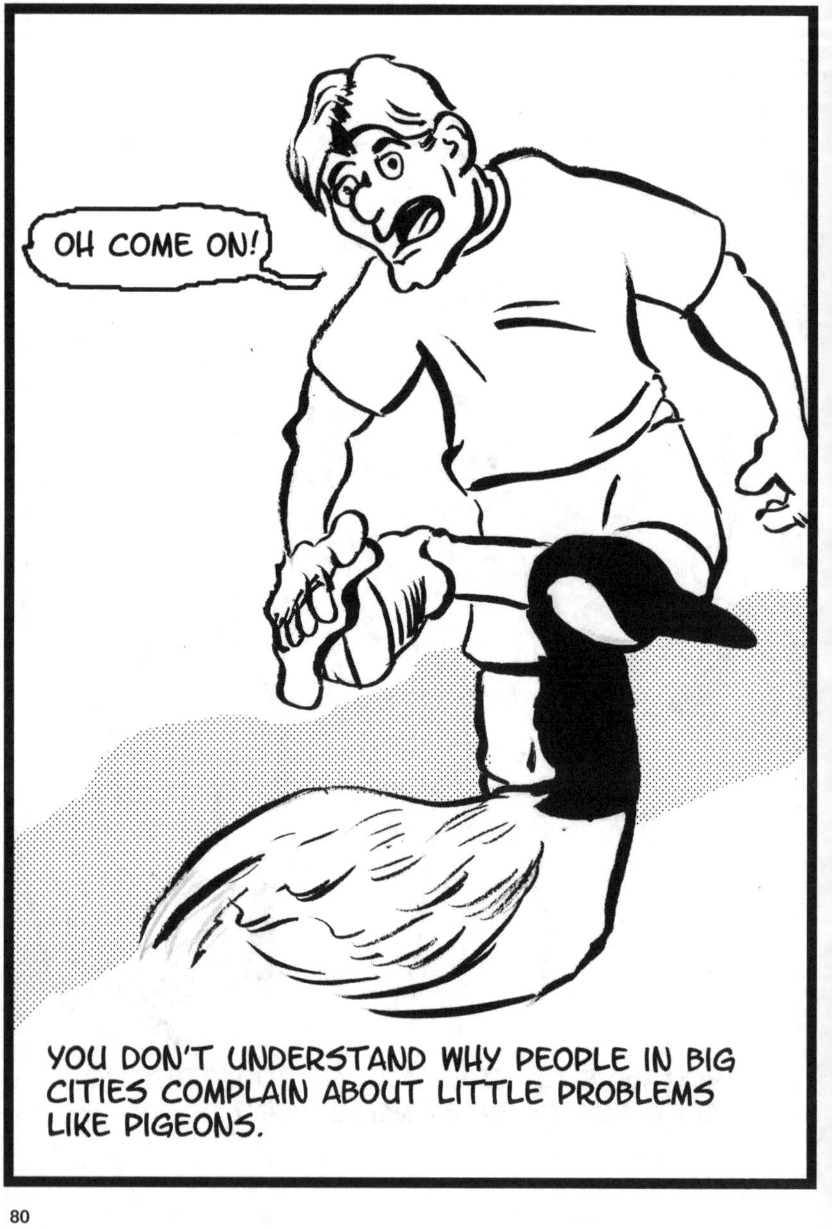
OH COME ON!
YOU DON'T UNDERSTAND WHY PEOPLE IN BIG CITIES COMPLAIN ABOUT LITTLE PROBLEMS LIKE PIGEONS.

YOU HAVE GOTTEN FROSTBITE WHILE
BARBECUING.

YOU STILL REMEMBER WHEN YOU SAW WHERE THE TREE LINE ENDS AND THE PRARIE BEGINS.

YOU HAVE HAD TO EXPLAIN TO VISITORS FROM OUT OF PROVINCE THAT YOU HAVE PAID TO WATCH CURLERS, NOT THE OTHER WAY AROUND.

YOU HAVE EVER HAD TO EXPLAIN WHY SOUTHEND IS IN THE NORTH AND EASTEND IS IN THE WEST.

YOU HAVE USED A GRANARY AS A SPARE ROOM.

85

WHEN YOU WERE A KID, THE T.V. SET HAD TWO CHANNELS: "CBC" AND OFF.

YOU LIVE IN A MAJOR CITY, AND YOU HAVE HAD TO YIELD FOR A MOOSE ON THE WAY TO WORK.

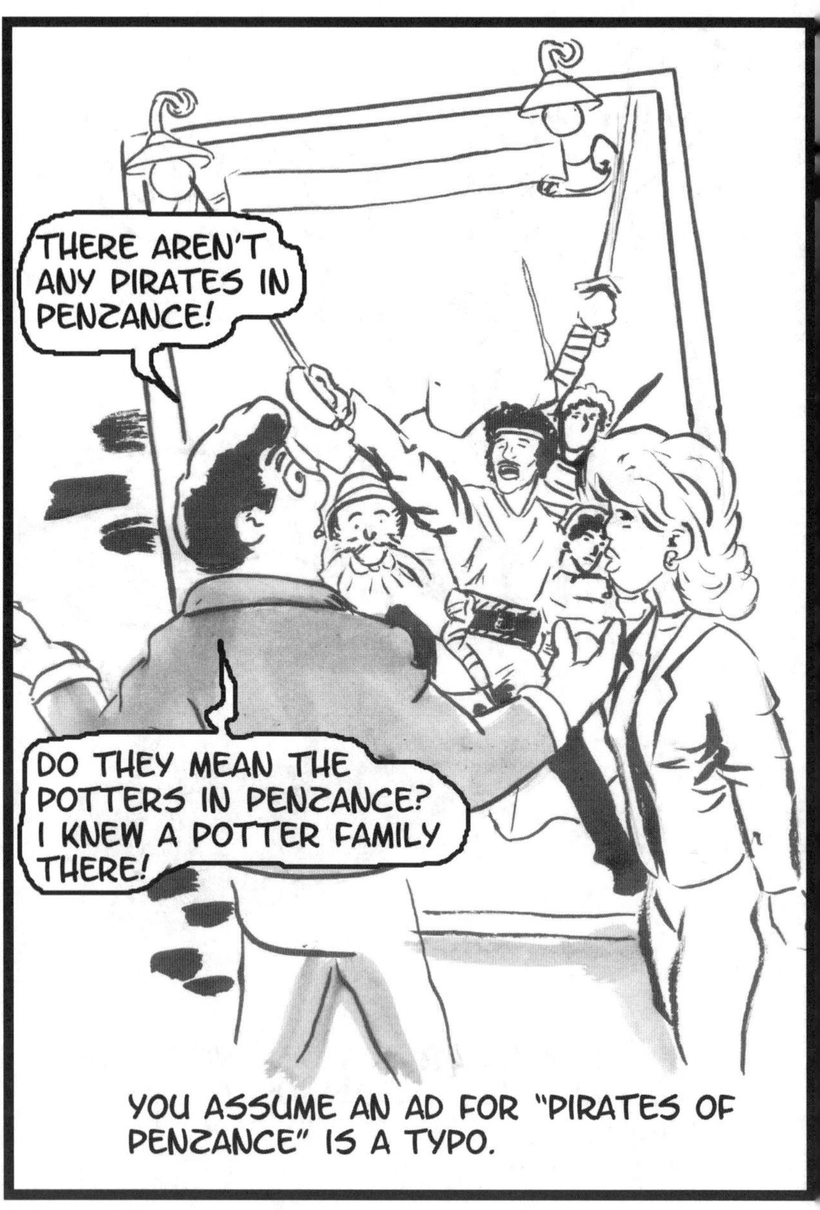
THERE AREN'T ANY PIRATES IN PENZANCE!
DO THEY MEAN THE POTTERS IN PENZANCE? I KNEW A POTTER FAMILY THERE!
YOU ASSUME AN AD FOR "PIRATES OF PENZANCE" IS A TYPO.

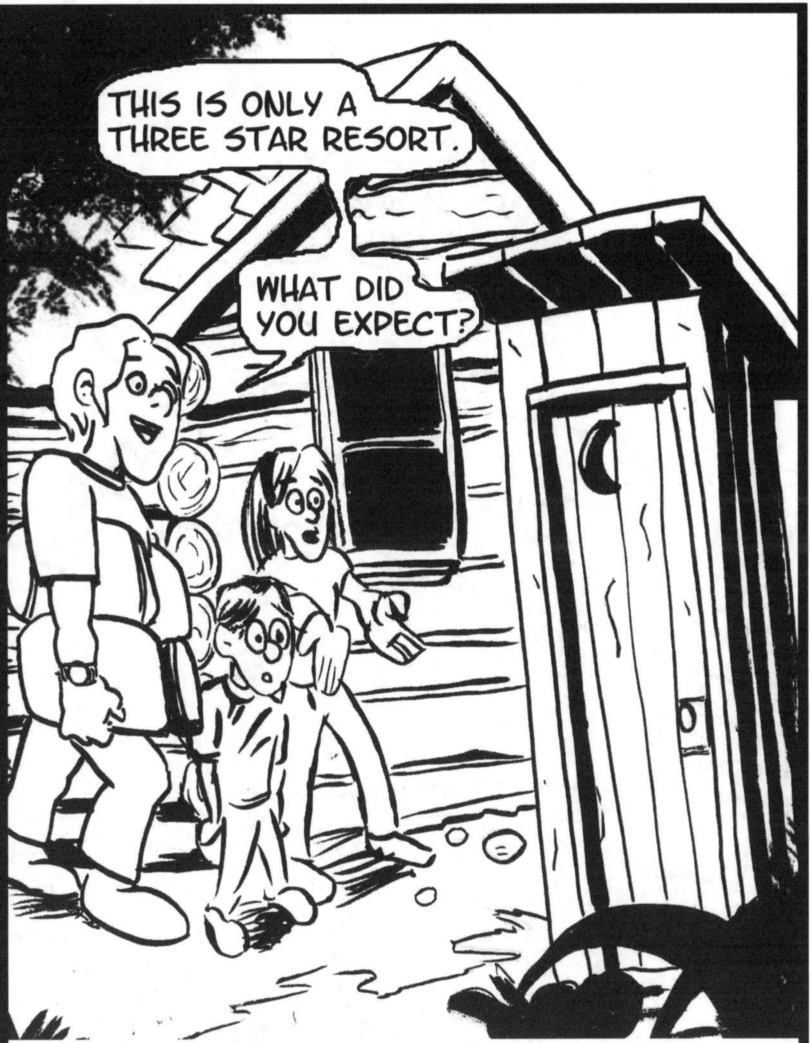
THIS IS ONLY A THREE STAR RESORT.
WHAT DID YOU EXPECT?

YOU CONSIDER A LUXURY VACATION RESORT IS ONE THAT HAS FLUSH TOILETS.

YOU HAVE BEEN TO AIRPORTS WHICH ARE NOT ONLY TOO SMALL TO LAND A JUMBO JET, THEY ARE SMALLER THAN A JUMBO JET.

YOU HAVE A FAMILY REUNION AND THE ENTIRE TOWN SHUTS DOWN.

R.I.P

YOU REMEMBER WHEN AN ELEVATOR WAS A
BUILDING, AND NOT SOMETHING IN A BUILDING.

YOU DON'T GO TO A GROCERY STORE OR A BANK, YOU GO TO THE CO-OP AND THE CREDIT UNION.

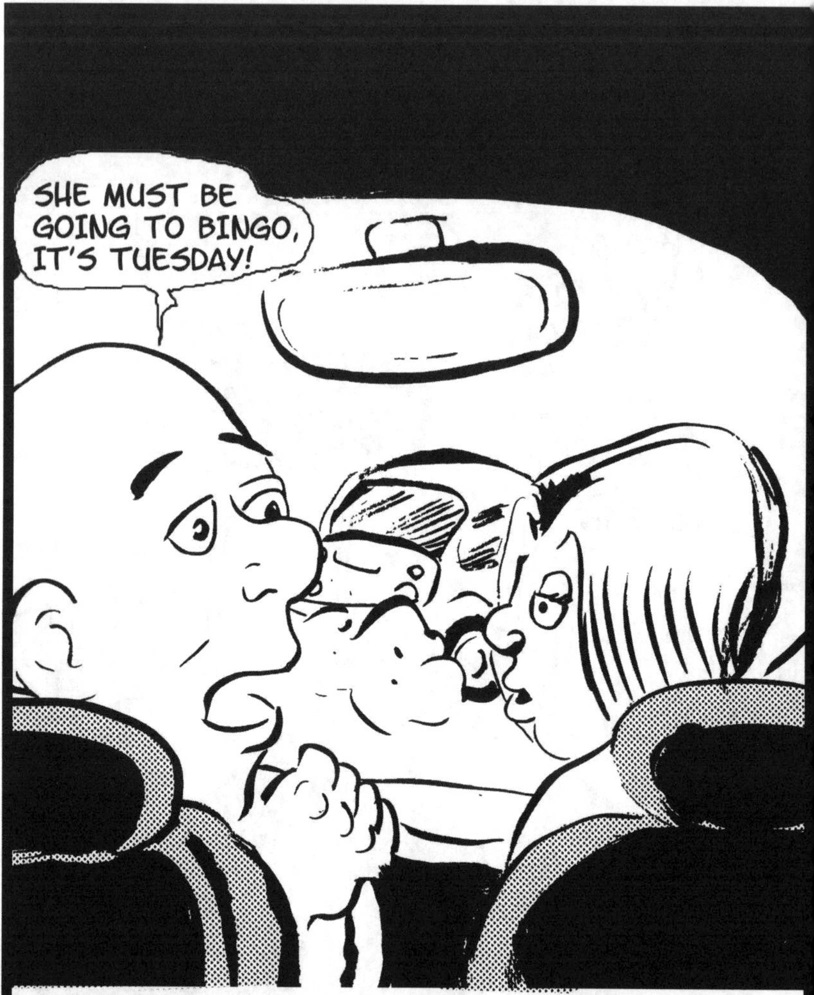
SHE MUST BE GOING TO BINGO, IT'S TUESDAY!
YOU DON'T USE TURN SIGNALS WHEN YOU DRIVE BECAUSE YOU ASSUME EVERYONE KNOWS WHERE YOU ARE GOING.

YOU DON'T DRIVE TO YOUR VACATION HOME, YOU DRIVE IN IT.

YOU HATE IT WHEN PEOPLE CALL FOWL SUPPERS "FOUL SUPPERS".

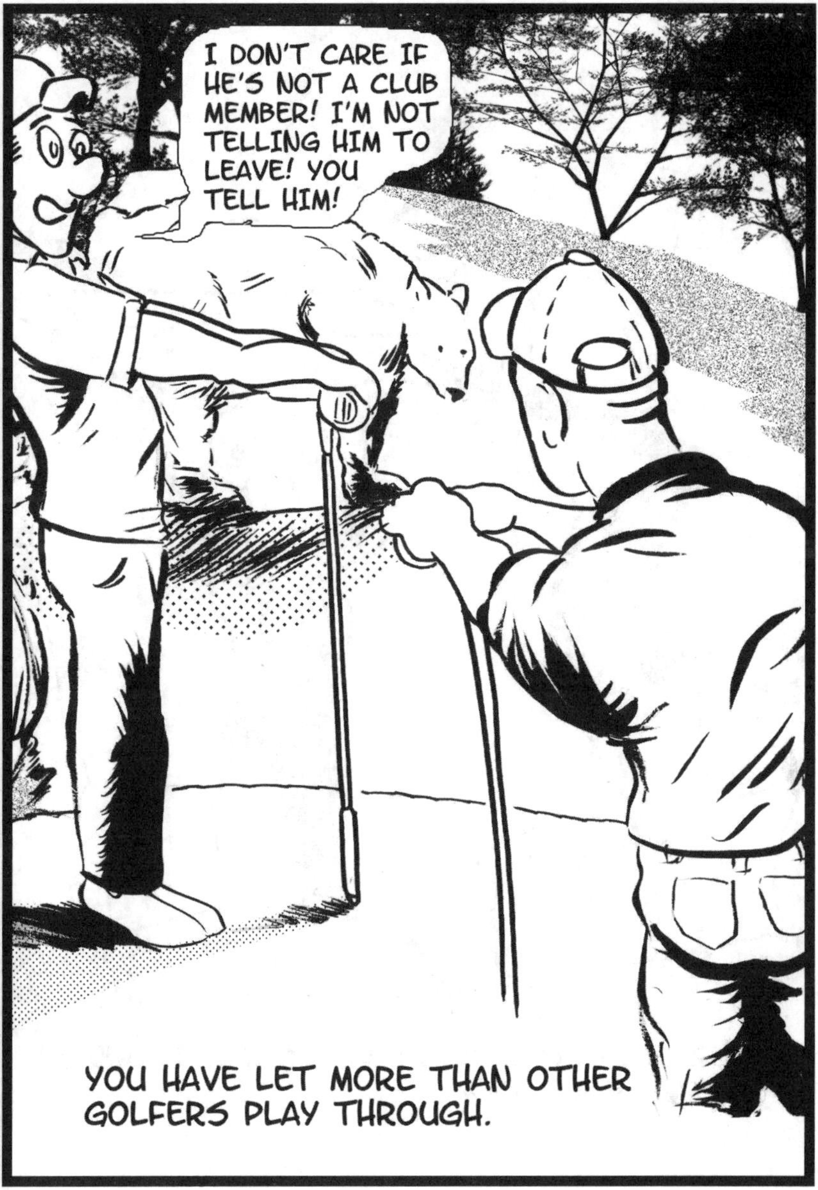
I DON'T CARE IF HE'S NOT A CLUB MEMBER! I'M NOT TELLING HIM TO LEAVE! YOU TELL HIM!
YOU HAVE LET MORE THAN OTHER GOLFERS PLAY THROUGH.

YOUR GOLF COURSE HAS RULES NOT FOUND IN THE PGA RULE BOOK.

YOU'RE FINE WITH STRIP BARS BEING ILLEGAL BUT YOU WISH THEY'D GET RID OF THAT IMMORAL LONG GUN REGISTRY.

YOU HAVE PANICKED IN A LIGHTNING STORM BECAUSE YOU REALIZED THAT YOU ARE THE HIGHEST POINT OF LAND AROUND.

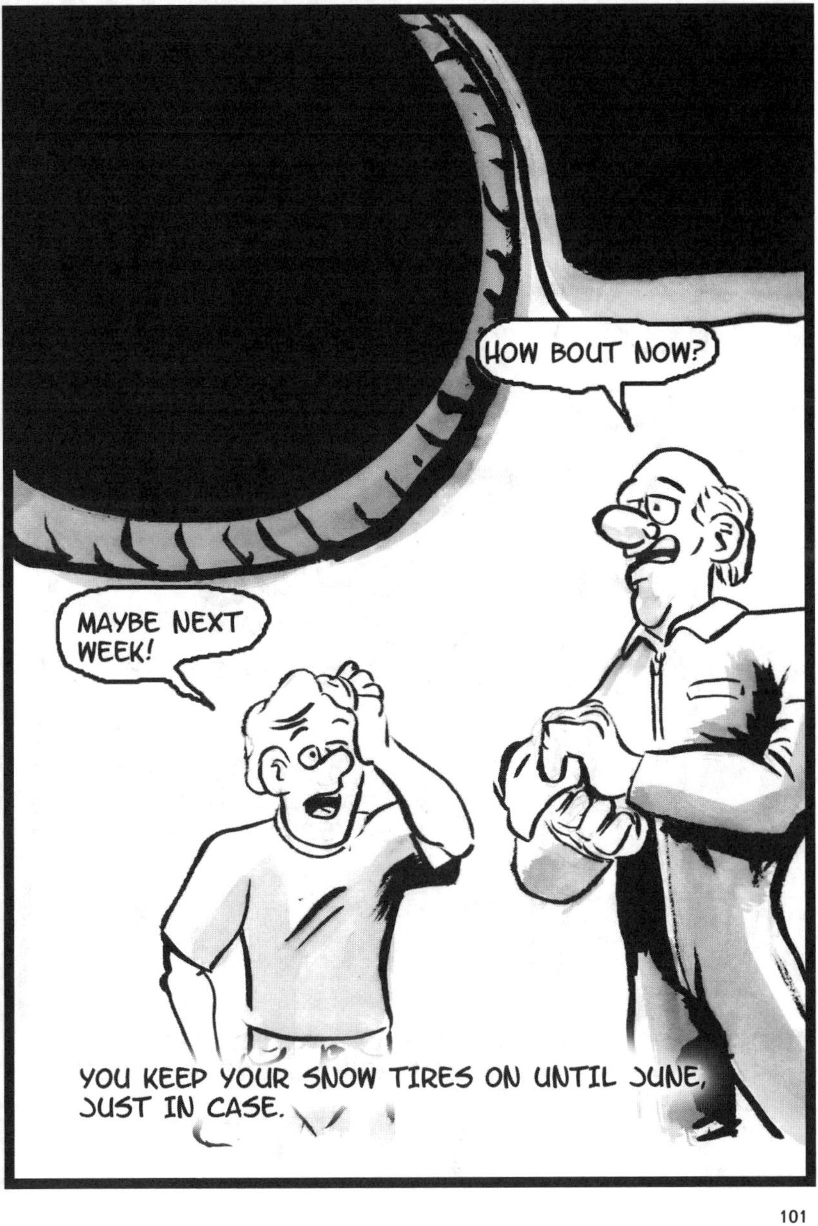
HOW BOUT NOW?
MAYBE NEXT WEEK!
YOU KEEP YOUR SNOW TIRES ON UNTIL JUNE, JUST IN CASE.

PROVINCE OF SASKATCHEWAN

CERTIFICATE OF LIVE BIRTH

BORN ON 10 DEGREES NORTH
BY 15 DEGREES SOUTHWEST
OF ROSETOWN.

SOMEONE IN YOUR FAMILY HAS A BIRTH CERTIFICATE
WHICH LISTS A LAND DESCRIPTION INSTEAD OF A HOSPITAL
AS THE LOCATION OF BIRTH.

"JOHN DEERE" IS YOUR FAVORITE FASHION DESIGNER, INTERIOR DECORATOR, AND TOY MANUFACTURER.

YOUR TANNING BED IS 100% ORGANIC.

YOUR TRAVEL TIME TO A FOOTBALL GAME EXCEEDS
THE ACTUAL GAME TIME.

YOUR POOR DOG STILL REMEMBERS THE TIME
YOU READ "THE DOG WHO WOULDN'T BE."

YOU GREW UP THINKING SANTA CLAUS
TRAVELLED BY TRAIN

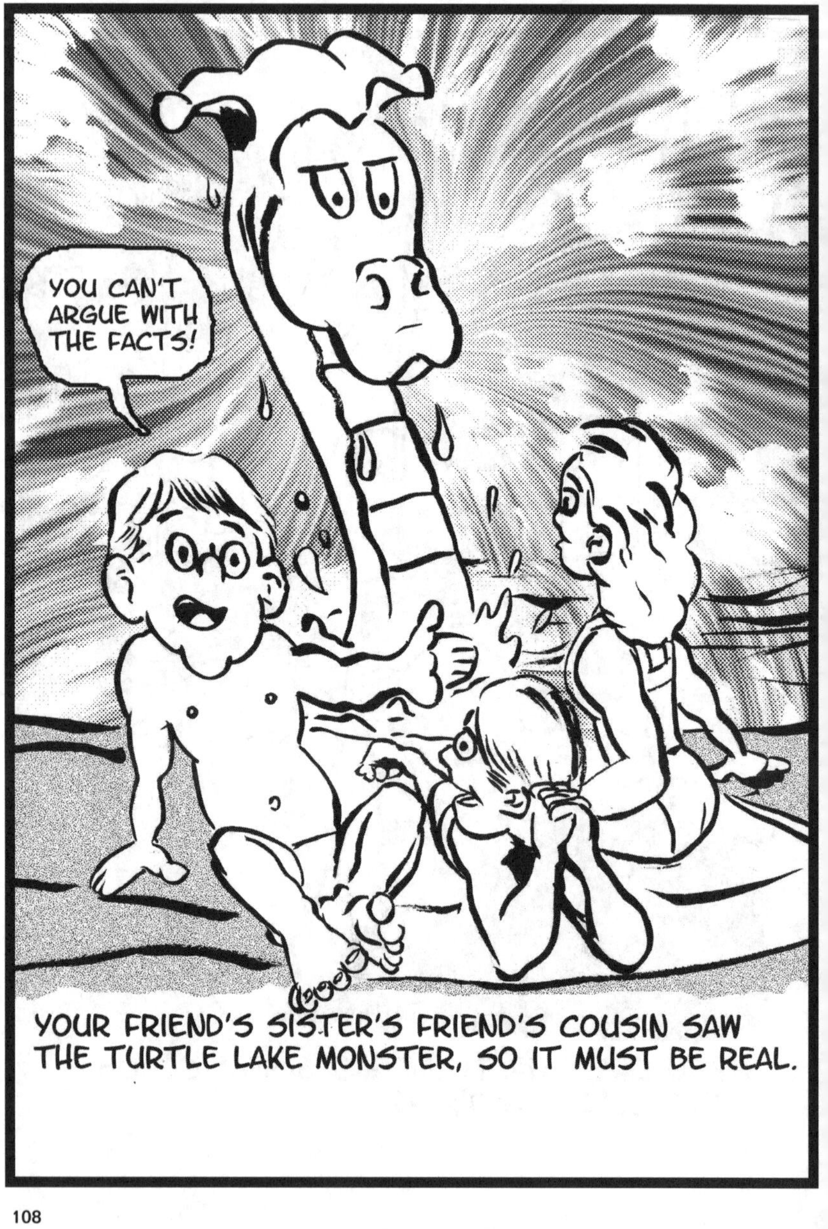
YOU CAN'T ARGUE WITH THE FACTS!

YOUR FRIEND'S SISTER'S FRIEND'S COUSIN SAW THE TURTLE LAKE MONSTER, SO IT MUST BE REAL.

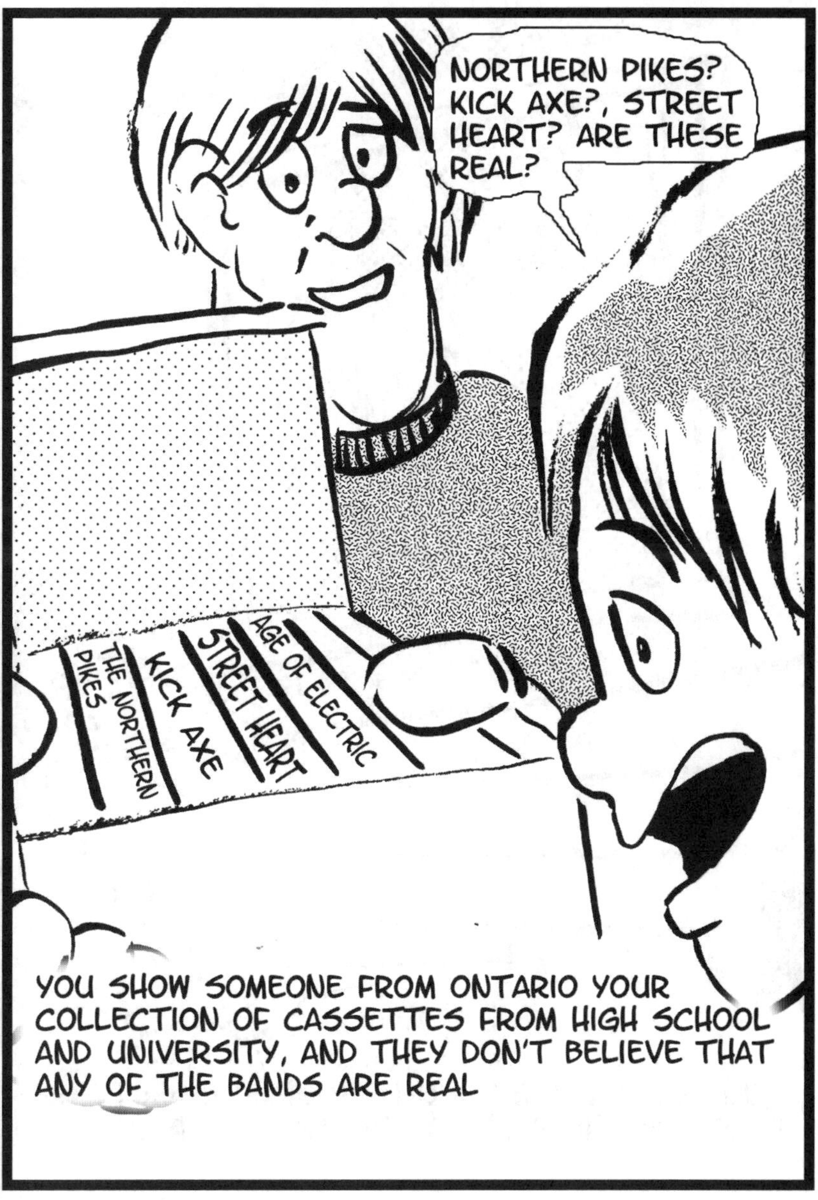
NORTHERN PIKES? KICK AXE?, STREET HEART? ARE THESE REAL?
AGE OF ELECTRIC
STREET HEART
KICK AXE
THE NORTHERN PIKES
YOU SHOW SOMEONE FROM ONTARIO YOUR COLLECTION OF CASSETTES FROM HIGH SCHOOL AND UNIVERSITY, AND THEY DON'T BELIEVE THAT ANY OF THE BANDS ARE REAL

YOU DON'T WORRY ABOUT YOUR KIDS GETTING LOST ON THE WAY TO THE SKATING RINK.

YOU ONLY FIND YOUR TURN SIGNAL IS BROKEN AFTER DRIVING FOR 3 HOURS, BECAUSE YOU TRAVELLED FOR 300 KILOMETERS WITHOUT TURNING.

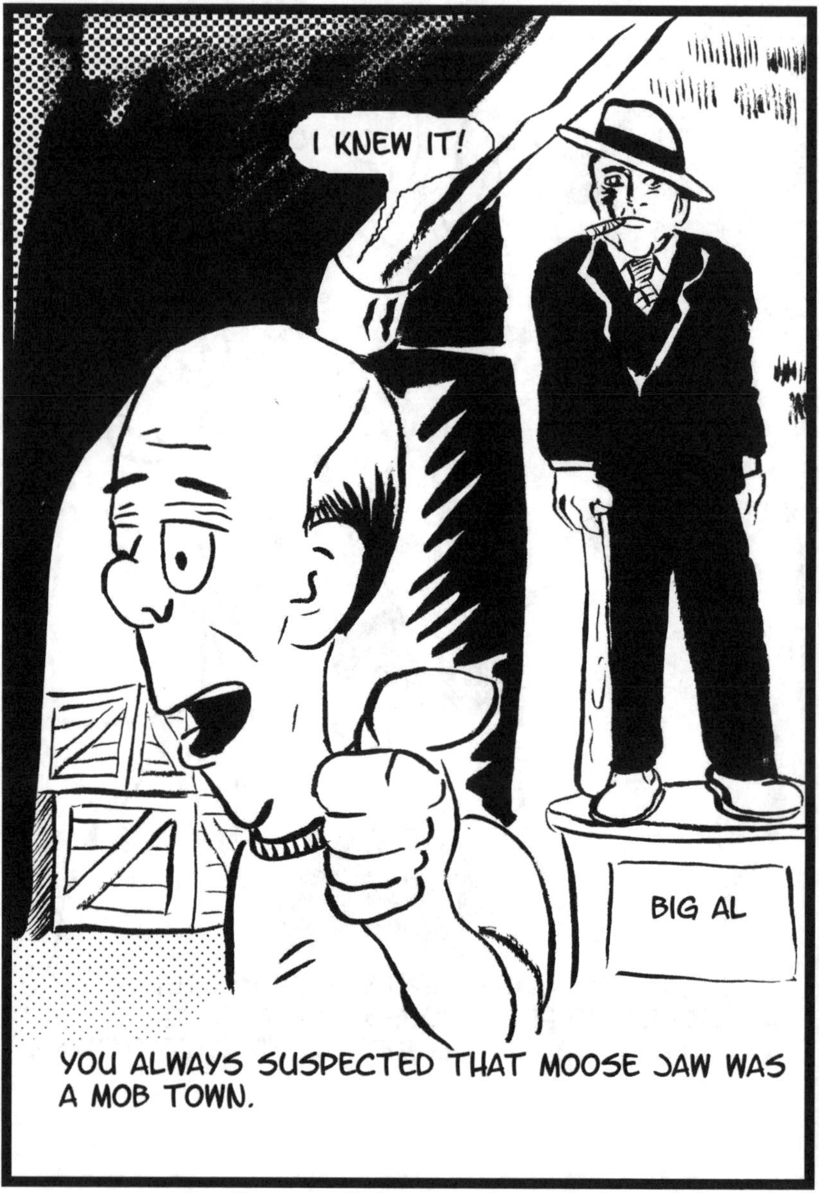
I KNEW IT!
BIG AL
YOU ALWAYS SUSPECTED THAT MOOSE JAW WAS A MOB TOWN.

SOMEONE IN THE THIRD GRADE TRICKED YOU INTO LICKING A PIECE OF POTASH AND YOU STILL REMEMBER WHAT IT TASTED LIKE.

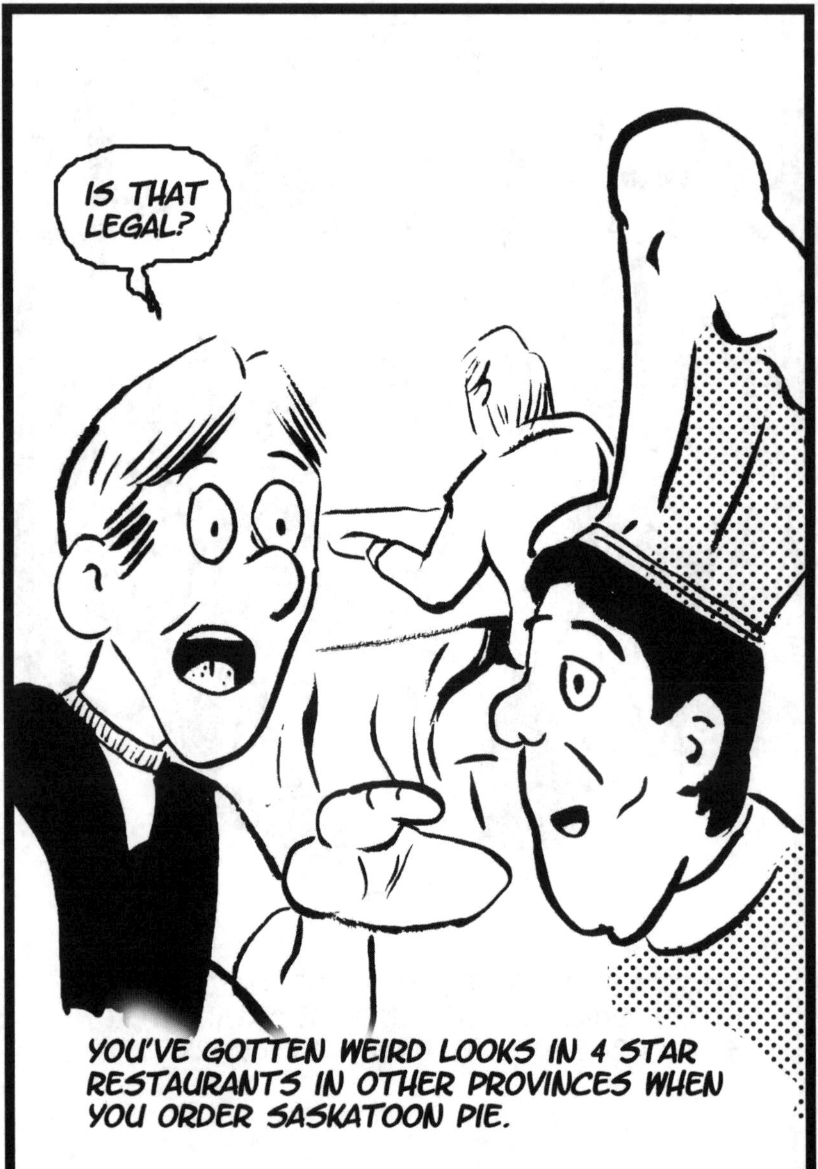
IS THAT LEGAL?
YOU'VE GOTTEN WEIRD LOOKS IN 4 STAR RESTAURANTS IN OTHER PROVINCES WHEN YOU ORDER SASKATOON PIE.

YOU DECORATE MORE THAN A TREE FOR CHRISTMAS.

YOUR ONLY NEW YEAR'S EVE WITHOUT SNOW WAS IN 1997, AND YOU REMEMBER IT LIKE IT WAS YESTERDAY.

YOUR LOCAL THEATRE DIDN'T PLAY "STAR WARS" UNTIL 1980.

SOMEONE IN YOUR FAMILY HAS A GREEN AND WHITE WARDROBE

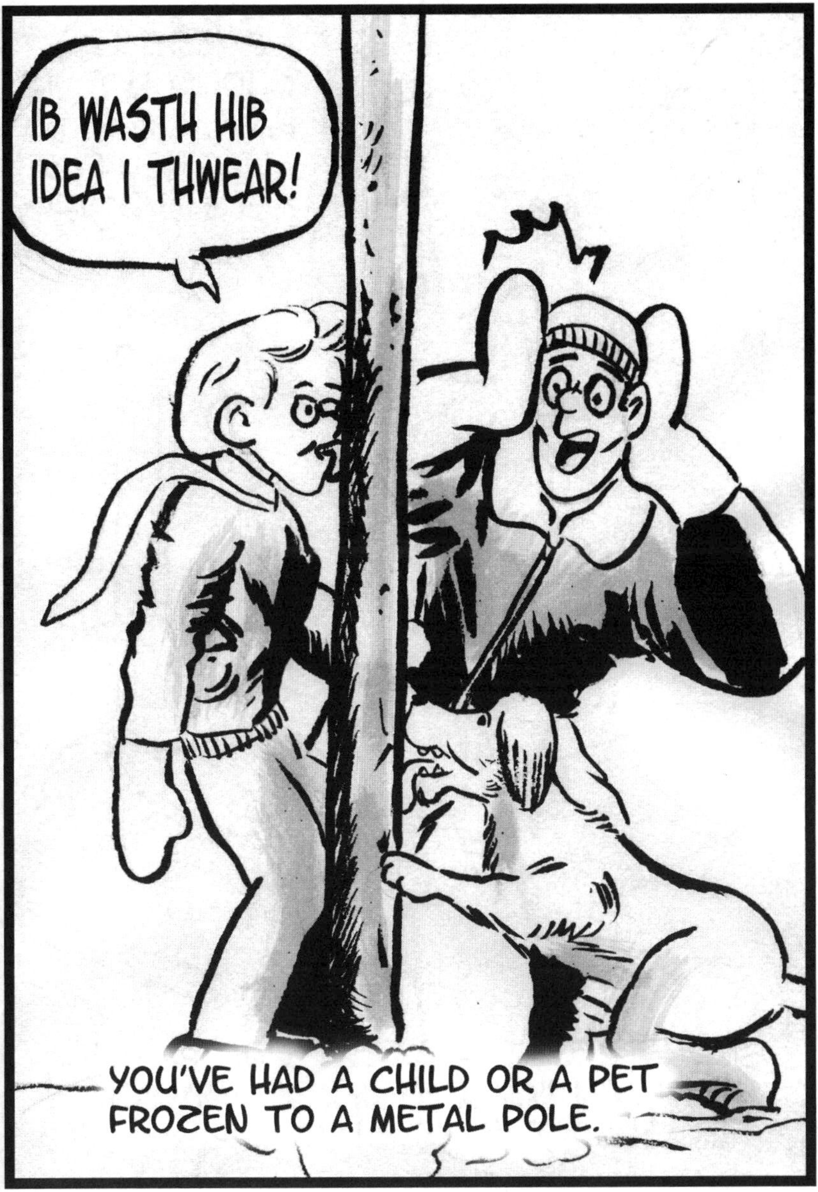
IB WASTH HIB IDEA I THWEAR!
YOU'VE HAD A CHILD OR A PET FROZEN TO A METAL POLE.

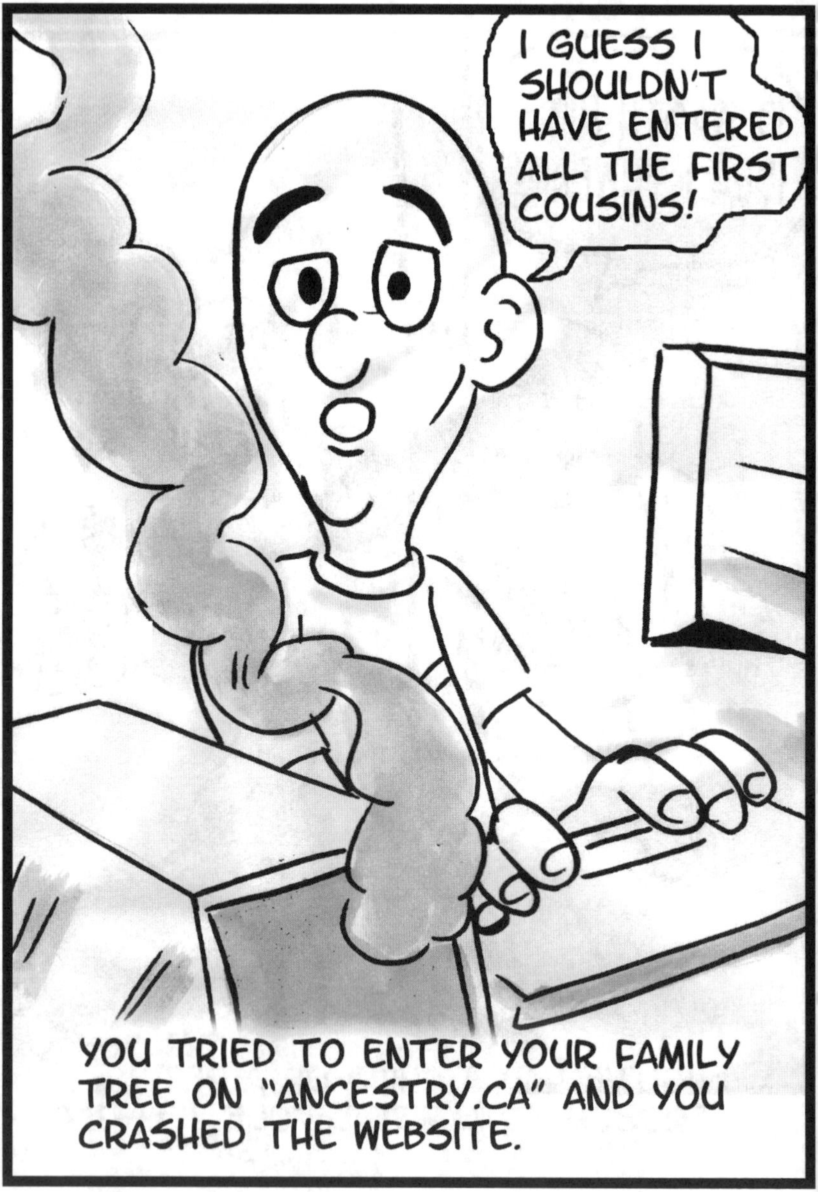
I GUESS I SHOULDN'T HAVE ENTERED ALL THE FIRST COUSINS!
YOU TRIED TO ENTER YOUR FAMILY TREE ON "ANCESTRY.CA" AND YOU CRASHED THE WEBSITE.

YOUR MOST EXPENSIVE BOOTS AREN'T
DESIGNER, THEY'RE STEEL-TOED.

YOU'VE HAD A GARDEN WITH MORE SQUARE FOOTAGE THAN YOUR HOUSE.

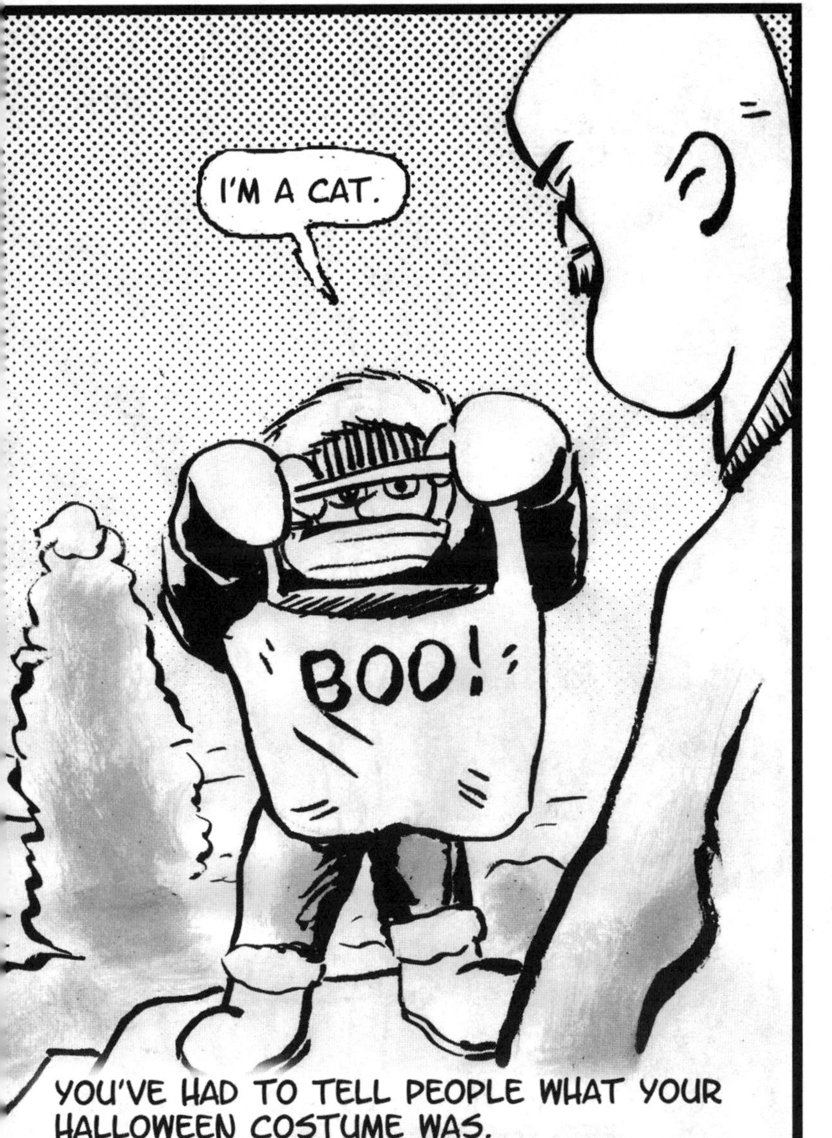
I'M A CAT.
BOO!
YOU'VE HAD TO TELL PEOPLE WHAT YOUR HALLOWEEN COSTUME WAS.

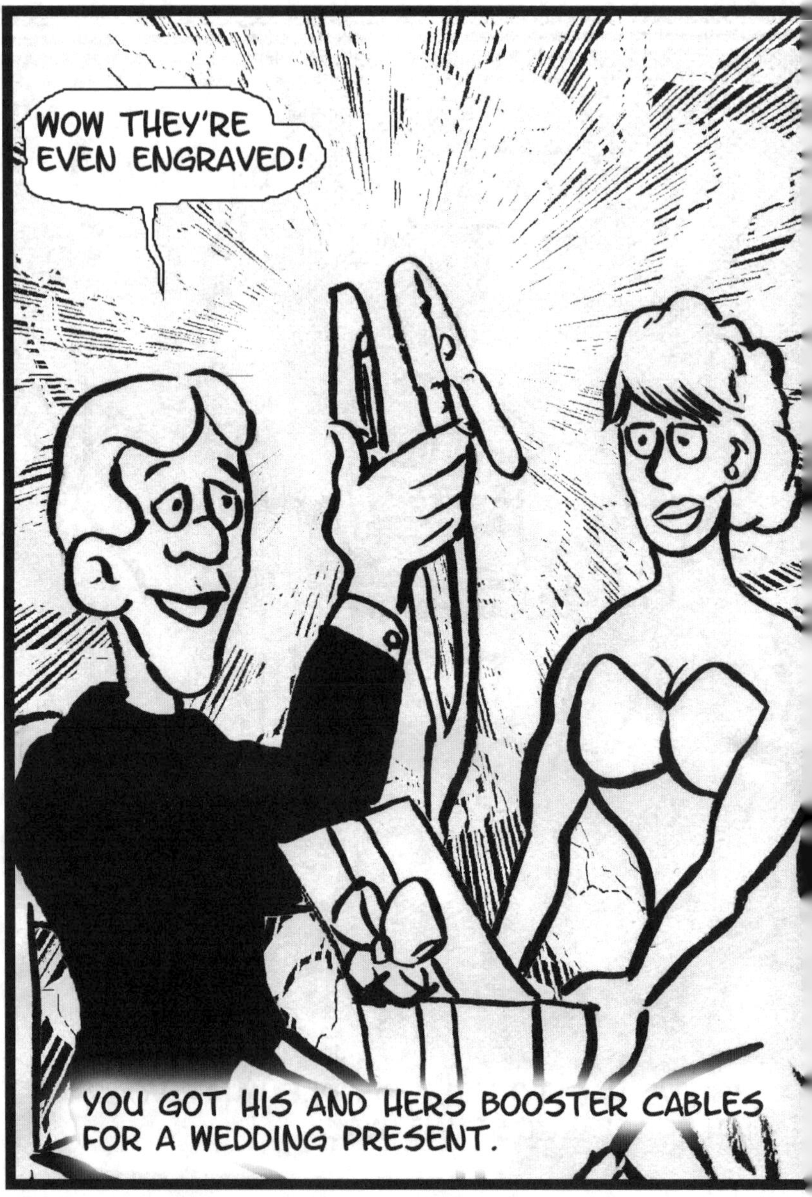
WOW THEY'RE EVEN ENGRAVED!
YOU GOT HIS AND HERS BOOSTER CABLES FOR A WEDDING PRESENT.

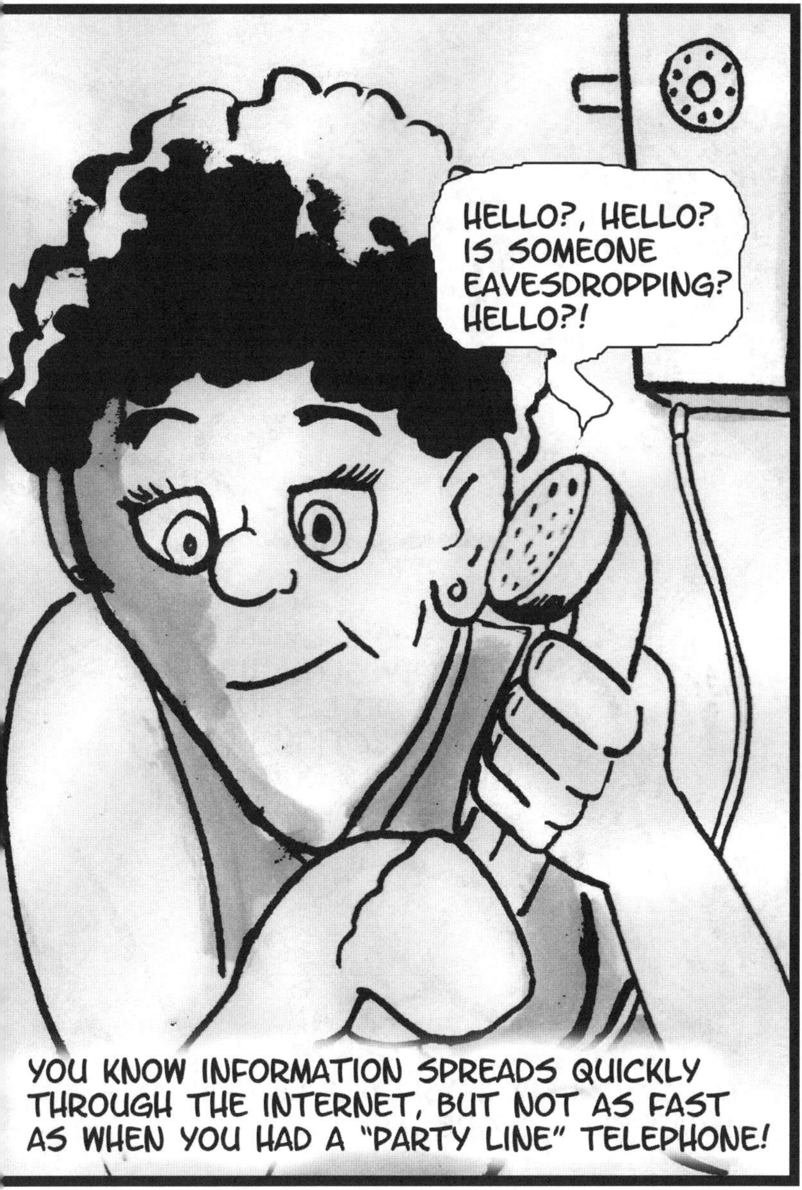
HELLO?, HELLO? IS SOMEONE EAVESDROPPING? HELLO?!
YOU KNOW INFORMATION SPREADS QUICKLY THROUGH THE INTERNET, BUT NOT AS FAST AS WHEN YOU HAD A "PARTY LINE" TELEPHONE!

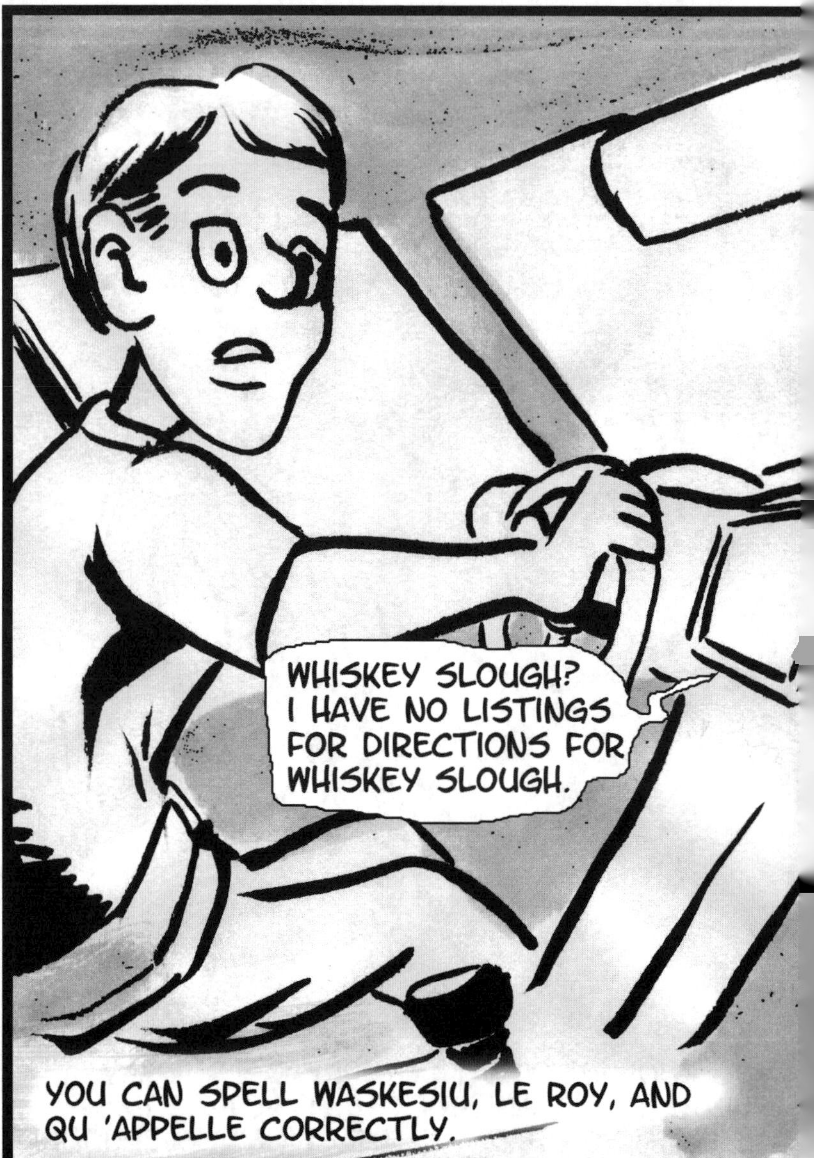
WHISKEY SLOUGH? I HAVE NO LISTINGS FOR DIRECTIONS FOR WHISKEY SLOUGH.
YOU CAN SPELL WASKESIU, LE ROY, AND QU 'APPELLE CORRECTLY.

A CROWD GATHERS WHEN THE LIBRARY GETS A NEW BOOK.

YOUR FAVORITE RESTAURANT SERVES GASOLINE AND MEALS.

A STORE CONTINUES TO BE A LAND MARK
LONG AFTER IT CLOSES.

YOU STOP IN A CITY YOU MOVED FROM 15 YEARS AGO, YOU STOP FOR A HAIR CUT AND THE BARBER ASKS IF YOU WANT THE USUAL.

YOU HAVE HEARD MORE RURAL LEGENDS THAN URBAN ONES.

YOUR LOCAL NEWS PAPER ONLY COMES OUT ONCE A WEEK, AND THEY STILL HAVE TROUBLE FINDING HEADLINES.

YOU'VE ACTUALLY HAD TO TRY THE OLD
WIVES TALE THAT TOMATO JUICE GETS
OUT SKUNK STINK.

YOU PUT MORE SALT ON YOUR SIDEWALK
THAN YOU DO ON YOUR FOOD.

YOU HAD TO WAIT FOR A CONCERT TO START BECAUSE THEY HAD TO TAKE THE ICE OUT OF THE HOCKEY RINK BEFORE THE BAND WENT ON.

YOUR CONVERTABLE STILL LOOKS BRAND NEW AFTER 20 YEARS, BECAUSE YOU HAVE ONLY BEEN ABLE TO DRIVE IT FOR 2 YEARS OF THAT TIME.

YOU WENT TO THE ONE AND ONLY ROLLING STONES CONCERT IN YOUR PROVINCE'S HISTORY, SO YOU COULD SEE THE CROWD. NOT THE STUPID BAND.

YOU'VE BOUGHT A DOG BASED ON HOW WARM IT WILL KEEP YOU AT NIGHT.

YOUR LOCAL AUTOBODY SHOP HAS VARIABLE RATES.

YOU THINK THAT BLT STANDS FOR BANNOCK, LETTUCE, AND TOMATO.

YOU DOUBT THE AUTHENTICITY OF YOUR LOCAL CHINESE RESTAURANT.

YOUR COFFEE TABLE BOOK IS A CATALOGUE

YOUR TOOLBOX HAS ONE ITEM

YOUR HAT, YOUR TRUCK AND YOUR UNDERWEAR
ALL HAVE FLAPS.

NOT ONLY IS THE "PACMAN" MACHINE FROM WHEN YOU WERE A KID STILL IN TOWN, BUT YOUR HIGH SCORE IS STILL ON IT.

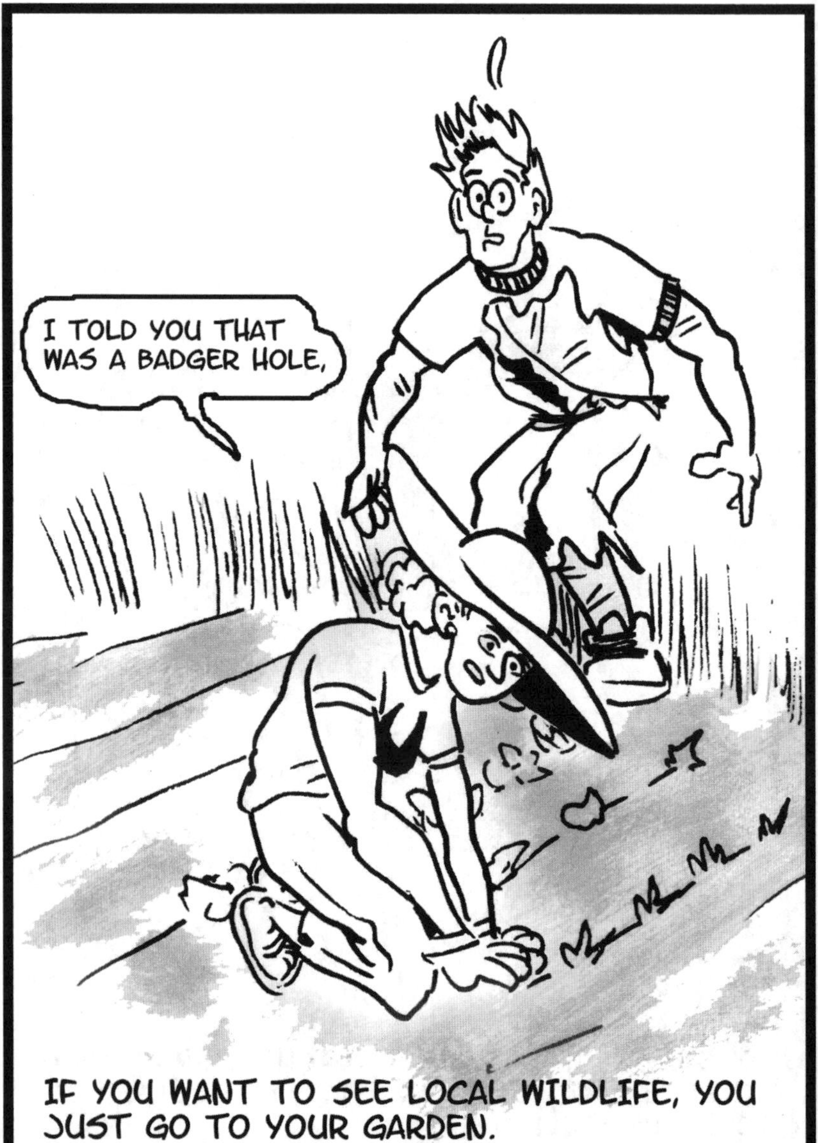
I TOLD YOU THAT WAS A BADGER HOLE,
IF YOU WANT TO SEE LOCAL WILDLIFE, YOU JUST GO TO YOUR GARDEN.

YOU HAVE EVER PLAYED TAG WITH A TUMBLEWEED.

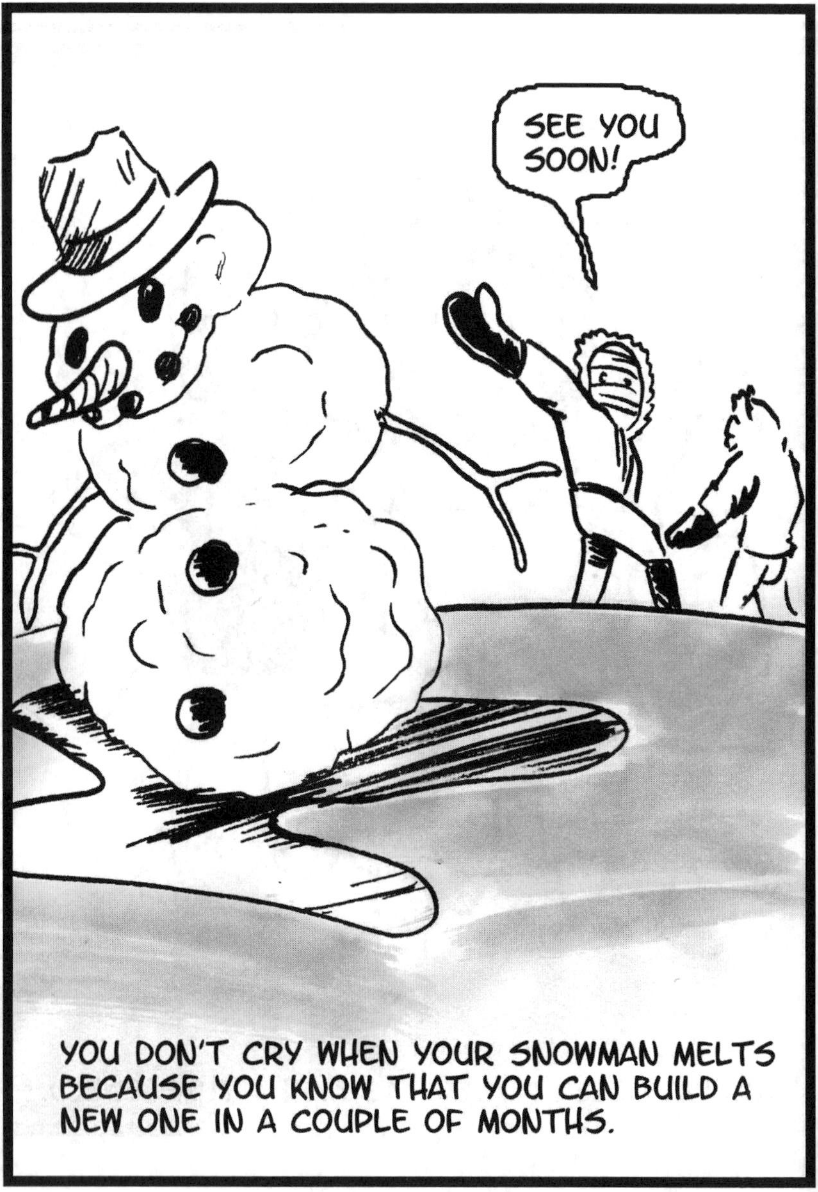
SEE YOU SOON!
YOU DON'T CRY WHEN YOUR SNOWMAN MELTS BECAUSE YOU KNOW THAT YOU CAN BUILD A NEW ONE IN A COUPLE OF MONTHS.

YOU WENT TO A SUMMER CAMP WITH UNUSUAL GAMES.

149

YOU'D RATHER HAVE THE WIND ON YOUR
SIDE THAN PICK THE FIRST PLAYER AT RECESS.

YOU HAVE OWNED A TRAILER WITH A LEVELLER FOR FIVE YEARS, AND YOU HAVE NEVER HAD TO USE IT.

YOU HATE HORROR MOVIES, BUT YOU SAW THE HALLOWEEN MOVIES BECAUSE SOMEBODY FROM SASKATOON WAS IN IT.

YOU HAVE ONE FAMILY MEMBER WHO REFUSES TO CONVERT TO METRIC.

YOU ENJOY TELLING PEOPLE AFTER THE FACT
WHAT THE SAUSAGE YOU SERVED WAS MADE OF

YOU ARE DEFINITLEY FROM SASKATCHEWAN IF READING THIS BOOK MAKES YOU WANT TO GO BACK.